Orangutans

Leo Statts

abdopublishing.com

Published by Abdo Zoom™, PO Box 398166, Minneapolis, Minnesota 55439. Copyright © 2017 by
Abdo Consulting Group, Inc. International copyrights reserved in all countries. No part of this book may be
reproduced in any form without written permission from the publisher. Abdo Zoom™ is a trademark and logo
of Abdo Consulting Group, Inc.

Printed in the United States of America, North Mankato, Minnesota
062016
092016

THIS BOOK CONTAINS
RECYCLED MATERIALS

Cover Photo: Sergey Uryadnikov/Shutterstock Images
Interior Photos: Creativa Images/Shutterstock Images, 1; Mariusz Prusaczyk/iStockphoto, 4, 6–7; iStockphoto, 5, 8–9,
14–15; Shutterstock Images, 8, 10–11, 12; Red Line Editorial, 11, 20 (left), 20 (right), 21 (left), 21 (right); Kate Capture/
Shutterstock Images, 13; Josef Friedhuber/iStockphoto, 16; Guenter Guni/iStockphoto, 17; Denys Kutsevalov/
Shutterstock Images, 18–19

Editor: Brienna Rossiter
Series Designer: Madeline Berger
Art Direction: Dorothy Toth

Publisher's Cataloging-in-Publication Data
Names: Statts, Leo, author.
Title: Orangutans / by Leo Statts.
Description: Minneapolis, MN : Abdo Zoom, [2017] | Series: Rain forest animals |
    Includes bibliographical references and index.
Identifiers: LCCN 2016941149 | ISBN 9781680791952 (lib. bdg.) |
    ISBN 9781680793635 (ebook) | ISBN 9781680794526 (Read-to-me ebook)
Subjects: LCSH: Orangutans--Juvenile literature.
Classification: DDC 597.88--dc23
LC record available at http://lccn.loc.gov/2016941149

Table of Contents

Orangutans

Orangutans are primates.
They have shaggy red hair.

4

They are the largest animals
in the world that live in trees.

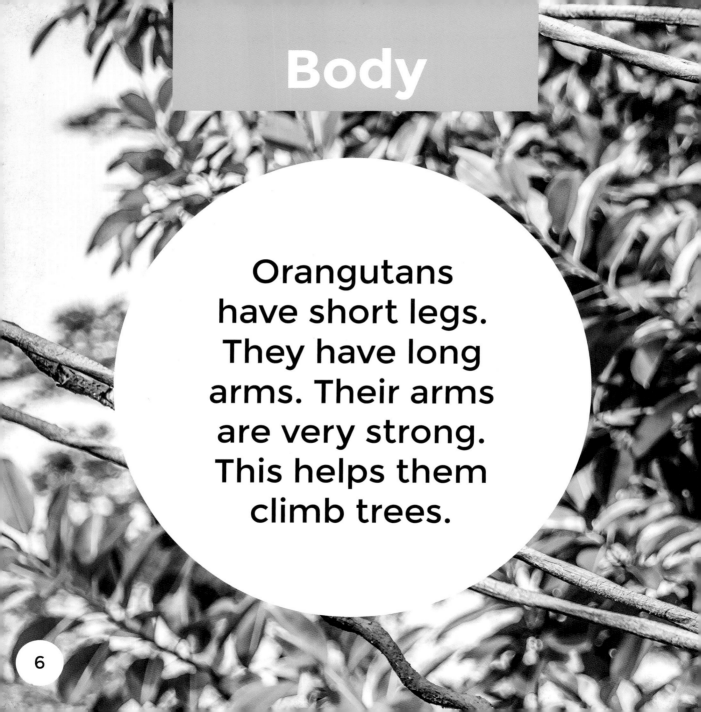

Body

Orangutans have short legs. They have long arms. Their arms are very strong. This helps them climb trees.

Orangutans use their fingers
to grab and hold.

Their feet can grab things, too.

Habitat

Orangutans live on two islands in Indonesia. One island is called Sumatra. The other is called Borneo.

Where orangutans live

Orangutans live in rain forests.

They spend most of their time
in trees. They swing from
branch to branch.

Food

Orangutans
are **omnivores**.
They mostly eat fruit.
They may also eat
eggs or bugs.

Life Cycle

Orangutans have
one baby at a time.

The baby lives with its mother
as long as seven years.

Adults usually live alone. They live up to 40 years in the wild.

Average Height

An orangutan is shorter than a door.

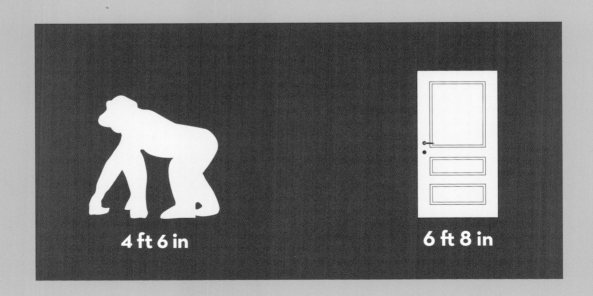

4 ft 6 in

6 ft 8 in

Average Weight

An orangutan is heavier than a toilet.

127 lbs   100 lbs

Glossary

omnivore - an animal that eats both plants and animals.

primate – a group of animals that includes humans, apes, and monkeys.

rain forest – a tropical woodland where it rains a lot.

shaggy - made up of long, tangled hair or fur.

Booklinks

For more information
on **orangutans**, please visit
booklinks.abdopublishing.com

Z∞m™ In on Animals!

Learn even more with the Abdo Zoom
Animals database. Check out
abdozoom.com for more information.

Index